图书在版编目（CIP）数据

哺乳动物 /（英）哥瑞斯·琼斯著；陈宇彤译 . —西安：世界图书出版西安有限公司，2018.1

（我的动物朋友）

ISBN 978-7-5192-3776-9

Ⅰ . ①哺…　Ⅱ . ①哥…　②陈…　Ⅲ . ①哺乳动物纲—青少年读物　Ⅳ . ① Q959.8-49

中国版本图书馆 CIP 数据核字（2017）第 276386 号

书　　名	**哺乳动物**（我的动物朋友）
著　　者	[英] 哥瑞斯·琼斯
译　　者	陈宇彤
策划编辑	陈宇彤
责任编辑	王　冰
装帧设计	新纪元文化传播
出版发行	**世界图书出版西安有限公司**
地　　址	西安市北大街 85 号
邮　　编	710003
电　　话	029-87214941　87233647（市场营销部） 029-87234767（总编室）
网　　址	http://www.wpcxa.com
邮　　箱	xast@wpcxa.com
经　　销	新华书店
印　　刷	鹤山雅图仕印刷有限公司
开　　本	787mm × 1092mm　1/12
印　　张	4
字　　数	20 千字
版　　次	2018 年 1 月第 1 版　2018 年 1 月第 1 次印刷
版权登记	25-2017-0062
国际书号	ISBN 978-7-5192-3776-9
定　　价	45.00 元

我的动物朋友

哺乳动物

[英]哥瑞斯·琼斯/著
陈宇彤/译

动物王国

世界图书出版公司
西安 北京 上海 广州

本书英文原版为英国国家图书馆馆藏图书。本书与英国、美国、加拿大三大英语系国家同步出版。

目录

什么是生物？

所有的生物都具有生长、发育、繁殖的能力。
生物需要空气、营养、水和阳光。

这些都是生物。

青蛙

老虎

人类

刀，叉，
盘子。

书

这些都是
非生物。

泰迪熊

非生物不具有生长、发育、繁殖的能力。非生物不需要空气、营养、水或阳光，因为它们没有生命气息。

什么是
哺乳动物？

哺乳动物是可以生活在水中，或陆地，或空中的生物。它们的生存离不开空气、食物、水和阳光。狮子、海豚和大象，都属于哺乳动物。

狮子

海豚

大象

哺乳动物呼吸空气，它们的身体表面通常会覆盖有毛发，且均有脊椎。它们是恒温动物，这就意味着，它们的体温不会随着外界温度的变化而变化。

北极熊即使在寒冷的环境下依然能够保持温暖，这是因为它们是恒温动物。

它们的栖息地

所有的生物都有它们的**栖息地**或家园。哺乳动物生活在世界各地许多不同的栖息地。一些哺乳动物生活在海洋、溪流、江河、湖泊等水域中。

其他哺乳动物则生活在遍布世界各地的沙漠、山脉和森林中。

热带雨林中的一只树懒。

哺乳动物的家园

某些哺乳动物，比如兔子，它们生活在地底下特别构建的家园中，我们称之为洞穴。它们的洞穴为它们躲避**捕食者**和寒冷的天气提供庇护。

阿曼沙漠中的
一只骆驼。

其他哺乳动物，比如骆驼，生活在**气候**炎热的地区，那里很少下雨。骆驼拥有宽蹄，这使得它们能够在沙子上轻松地行走而不会下陷。此外，骆驼可以在没水的情况下生存数月。

它们的食性

成年哺乳动物进食肉类或植物，或是两者混食。一些肉食性哺乳动物，比如老虎，有着长长的牙齿，称为犬齿，帮助它们把**猎物**撕成小块。

资料：

老虎是最大的大型猫科动物。

其他草食性哺乳动物，如奶牛，它们拥有四个胃，这使得它们能够吸收所食草中的**营养**。

它们如何呼吸？

所有哺乳动物通过它们的肺呼吸空气中的氧气。与小型哺乳动物相比，大型哺乳动物呼吸频率较低。

资料：

鲸鱼可以呆在水下两小时不呼吸。

生活在水中的哺乳动物（水生哺乳动物），比如鲸和海豚，它们通过它们头顶的鼻孔，也称作呼吸孔，来进行呼吸。

它们如何行动？

哺乳动物的行动方式取决于它们的生活环境。那些生活在热带雨林中的哺乳动物，通常拥有帮助它们保持平衡的尾巴，以及抓住树木的脚趾。

其他哺乳动物，比如蝙蝠，它们能够飞到树上，在那里有它们需要寻作食物的果实和昆虫。

它们如何生长？

大多数哺乳动物在它们出生前，它们的生命历程是以胎儿的形式在它们妈妈的身体里开始的。一些哺乳动物一胎生一个幼崽，有的则多达15个。

哺乳动物在它们成长及长成至成年期间，以母乳为食。
这个过程需要经历几个月甚至几年的时间。

不可思议的

哺乳动物

哺乳动物是世界上最聪明的动物。大象是世界上包括人类在内的，拥有最大大脑的哺乳动物。它们甚至能够记得多年前发生的事情。

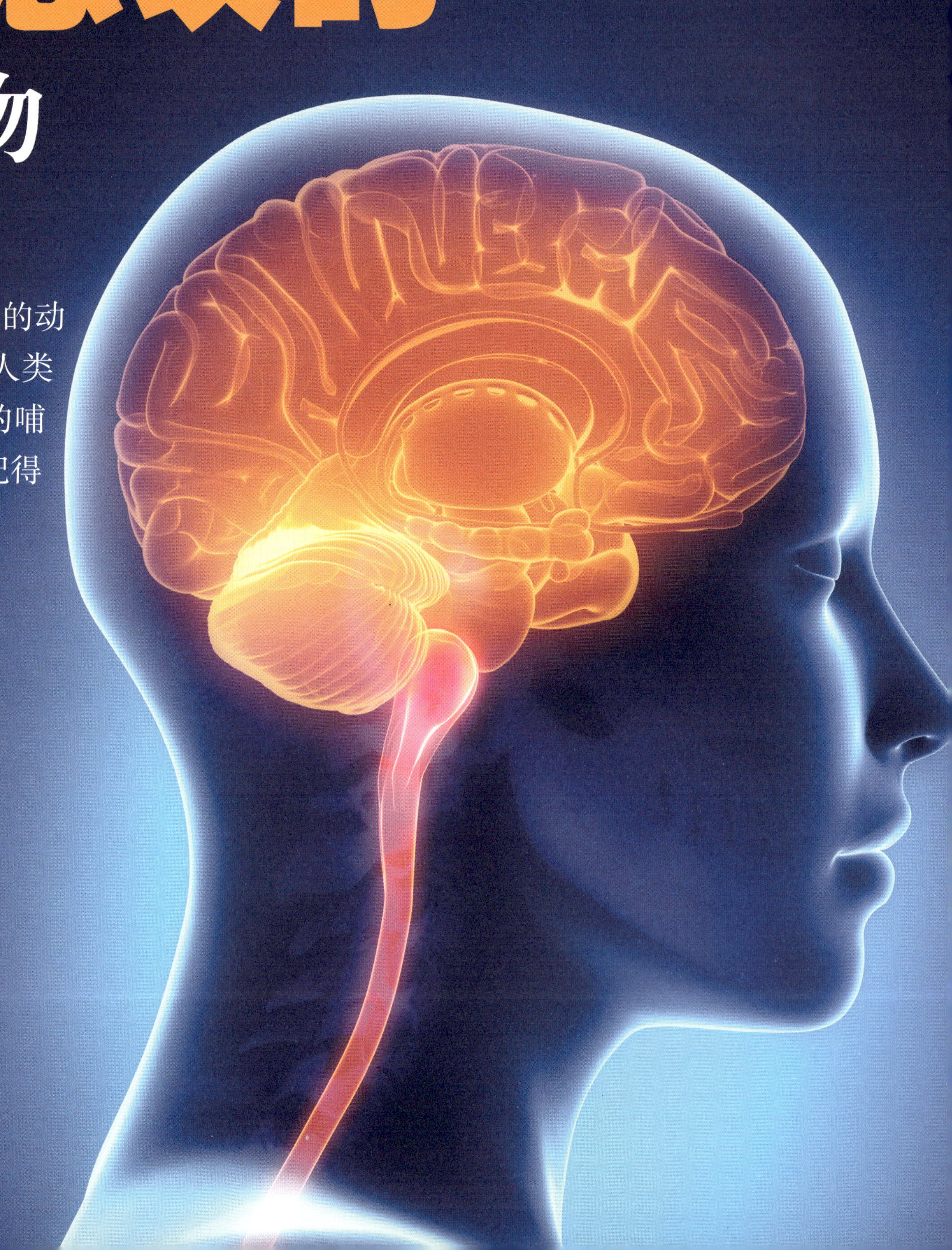

群居类哺乳动物在外通常彼此互相帮助。猫鼬是群居类哺乳动物，有的猫鼬群中猫鼬的数量可达50只。它们通常会在其他成年猫鼬外出寻找食物时，留下一只成年猫鼬照看幼崽。

猫鼬

打破世界纪录的
哺乳动物

蓝鲸

尺寸：
身体可
长达
30米

纪录：
世界上
最大的
哺乳动物

资料：
蓝鲸被认为是地球上生存过的体型最大的动物。仅蓝鲸的舌头就具有与大象体重一样的重量。

长颈鹿

纪录：

世界上
最高的
哺乳动物

尺寸：

身体高达
6米

资料：

幼年长颈鹿甚至
都比大多数成年
人高。

MAMMALS

Grace Jones

ANIMAL KINGDOM

世界图书出版公司
西安 北京 上海 广州

Words that appear like **this** can be found in the glossary on page 24.

Contents

A catalogue record for this book is available from the British Library.

What Are Living Things?

All living things have the ability to grow, develop and reproduce. Living things need air, nutrition, water and sunlight to stay alive.

These are all living things.

Frog

Tiger

Human

Knife, fork & plate.

Books

These are all non-living things.

Non-living things do not have the ability to grow, develop and reproduce. Non-living things do not need air, nutrition, water or sunlight because they are not alive.

Teddy Bear

What Is a Mammal?

Mammals are living things that can live in the water, or on land, or in the sky. They need air, food, water and sunlight to live.
Lions, dolphins and elephants are all types of mammal.

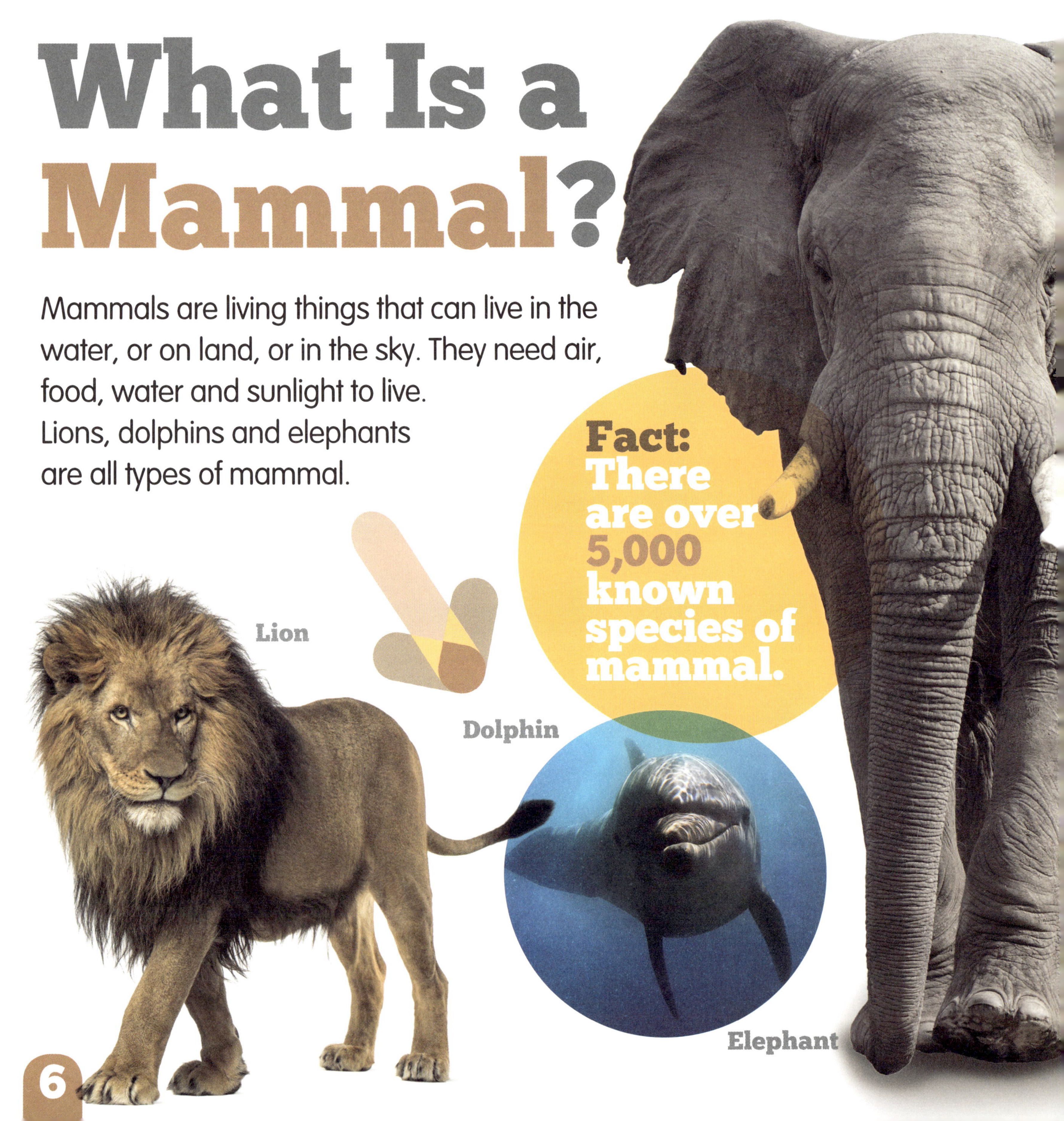

Fact: There are over 5,000 known species of mammal.

Lion

Dolphin

Elephant

Mammals breathe air, they usually have hair on their bodies and they all have a backbone. They are warm-blooded animals. This means that their body temperature does not change when the temperature does.

A polar bear stays warm even when it is freezing cold because it is warm-blooded.

Where Do They Live?

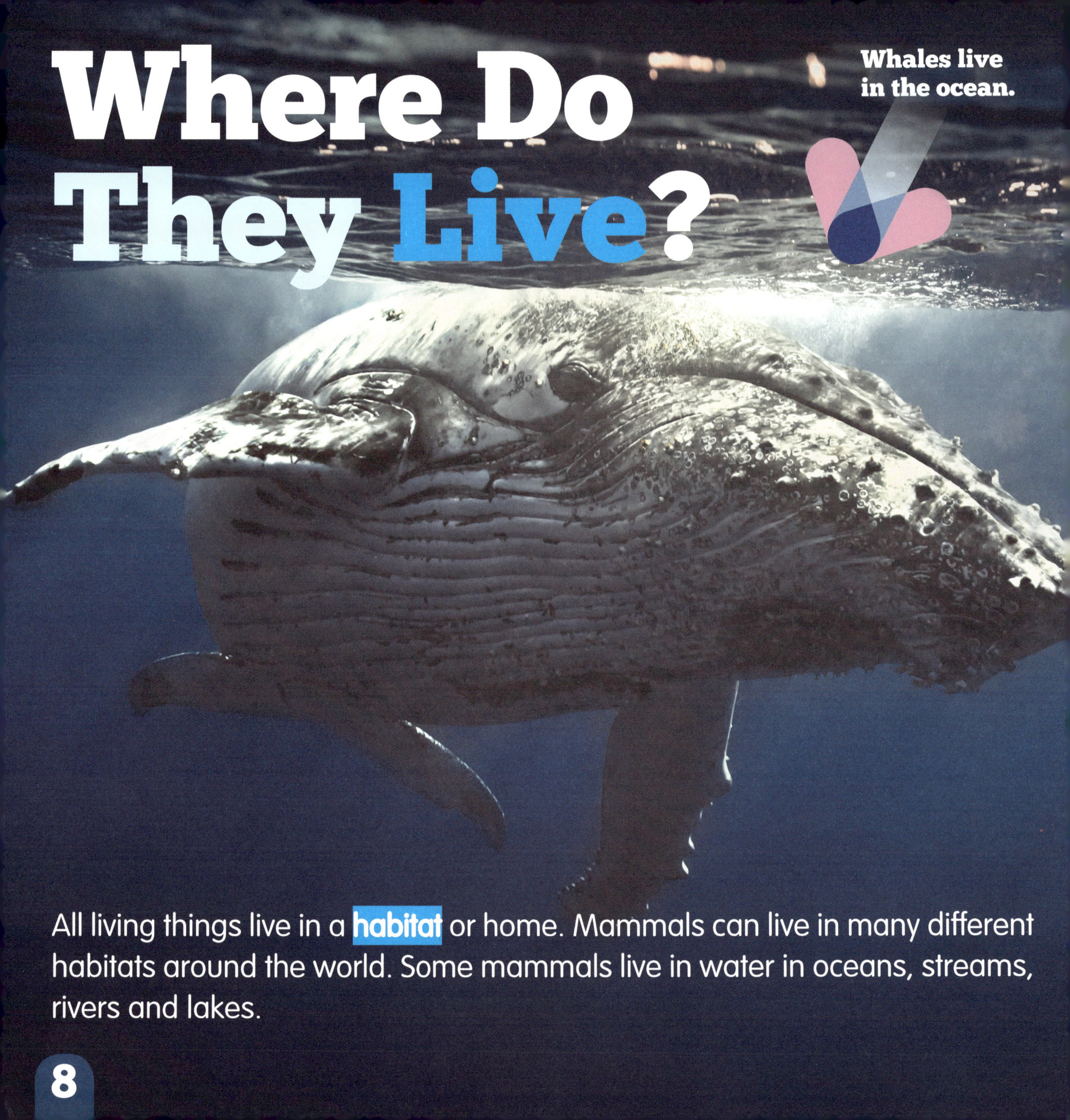

Whales live in the ocean.

All living things live in a **habitat** or home. Mammals can live in many different habitats around the world. Some mammals live in water in oceans, streams, rivers and lakes.

Other mammals live on land in the many deserts, mountains and forests that are found throughout the world.

A sloth in the rainforest.

Mammal Homes

Some mammals, like rabbits, live under the ground in specially built homes called burrows. Their burrows provide them with shelter from **predators** and the cold weather.

A camel in a desert in Oman.

Other mammals, such as camels, live in habitats that have hotter **climates** which get very little rain. Camels have wide hooves, so they can walk on sand easily without sinking. Besides, camels can survive for many months without water.

What Do They Eat?

Adult mammals eat meat or plants, or a mixture of both. Some mammals that eat meat, like tigers, have long teeth, called canines, which help them to tear their **prey** into smaller pieces.

Fact: Tigers are the largest of the big cats.

Other plant-eating mammals, like cows, have four stomachs so they can take in all the **nutrients** from the grass that they eat.

How Do They Breathe?

All mammals breathe in oxygen in the air through their lung. Larger mammals need to breathe less often than smaller mammals.

Fact:
A whale can stay under the water for two hours without breathing.

Mammals that live in water, like whales and dolphins, breathe in and out through nostrils on the top of their heads, called blowholes.

How Do They Move?

The way mammals move depends on the habitat they live in. Mammals who live in the trees of rainforests will often have tails to help them balance and toes that they use to grip trees with.

Fruit Bat

Other mammals, like bats, are able to fly so they can reach trees where the fruit and insects they feed on are found.

How Do They Grow?

Most mammals start life as babies inside their mother's body before they are born. Some mammals have one baby and others have as many as fifteen.

The babies feed on their mother's milk while they are still growing and changing into an adult. This can take anywhere from a few months to many years.

Marvellous Mammals

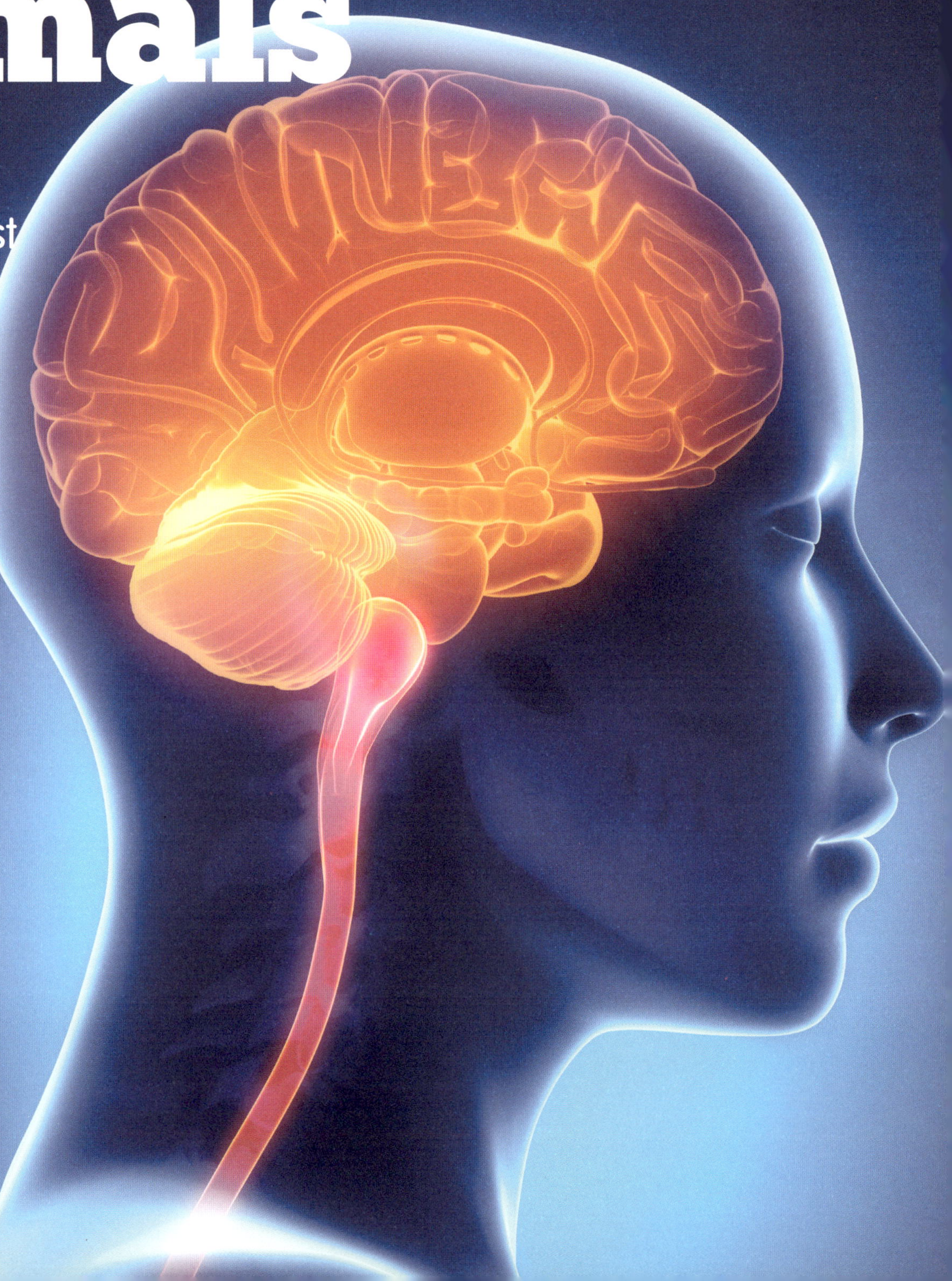

Mammals are the smartest animals in the world. The elephant has the largest brain of all mammals, including humans. They can still remember things that happened many years ago.

Mammals living in groups usually help each other out. Meerkats live in groups called colonies, which can include as many as fifty meerkats. They will normally have one babysitter who looks after the young when other adults are looking for food.

Meerkats

World Record Breakers

BLUE WHALE

Size: Up to 30 metres long

Record: The World's Biggest Mammal

Fact: The blue whale is the largest animal to have ever lived. Its tongue alone can weigh as much as an elephant!

GIRAFFE

Record: The World's Tallest Mammal

Size: Up to 6 metres long

Fact: Even baby giraffes are taller than most adult humans.

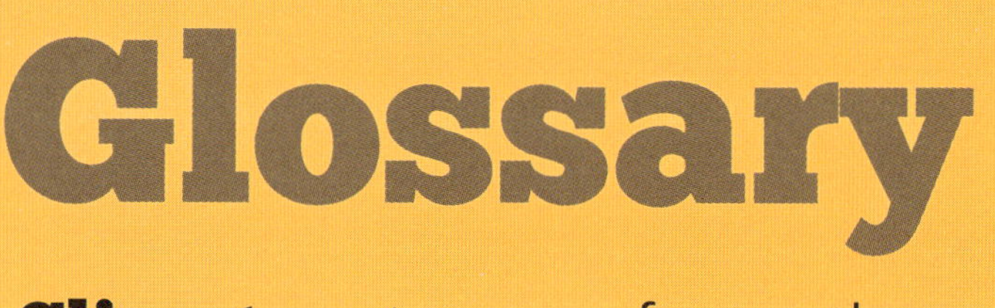

Glossary

Climates: types of weather in a particular place.

Habitat: a home where animals and plants live.

Nutrients: food needed for growth and health.

Predators: any animal that eats other animals and insects.

Prey: any animal or insect that is eaten by another.

Index

Photo Credits

Photocredits: Abbreviations: l-left, r-right, b-bottom, t-top, c-centre, m-middle. All images are courtesy of Shutterstock.com.

Front Cover-秋枫. 1,6r-Donovan van Staden. 2-3-Eric Gevaert. 4bl-Chros. 4c-Eric Isselee. 4r-michaeljung. 5bl-Elena Schweitzer. 5tl-koosen. 5r-Lichtmeister. 6bl-Eric Isselee. 6bc-Willyam Bradberry. 7-Tom linster. 8-Seb c'est bien. 9-nattanan726. 10-Ng Yin Jian. 11-Wolfgang Zwanzger. 12-Michal Ninger. 13-Dudarev Mikhail. 14-Szasz-Fabian Jozsef. 15-Christian Musat. 16-Ondrej Prosicky. 17-Ivan Kuzmin. 18-Linn Currie. 19-秋枫. 20-Custom media. 21-tratong. 22-powell'sPoint. 23-E. O. 24-ehtesham. 25-Oleg Znamenskiy.

ANIMAL KINGDOM

What is a living thing? Where do animals live? What do animals eat? How do they move and grow?

Learn the answers to these questions in this exciting new series. With easy to read text and informative diagrams, this series offers a simple introduction to the animals that live in our world.